31 Things to Raise a Child's Self-esteem

To our families and all the people who have touched our lives, and to all the young people who deserve to feel good about themselves as well as the parents who love them.

31 Things to Raise a Child's Self-esteem

Edie Hand and Dr. Judy Kuriansky

TRADE PAPER
PRESS

Turner Publishing Company
200 4th Avenue North • Suite 950
Nashville, Tennessee 37219
(615) 255-2665

www.turnerpublishing.com

31 Things to Raise a Child's Self-esteem

Library of Congress Cataloging-in-Publication Data

Hand, Edie, 1951-
 31 things to raise a child's self-esteem / Edie Hand and Judy Kuriansky.
 p. cm.
 ISBN 978-1-59652-582-5
1. Self-esteem in children. I. Kuriansky, Judith. II. Title. III. Title: Thirty-one things to raise a child's self-
esteem.
 BF723.S3H36 2010
 649'.7--dc22
 2010010255

Printed in China

10 11 12 13 14 15 16 17—0 9 8 7 6 5 4 3 2 1

Oft-times nothing profits more
Than self-esteem, grounded on just and right
Well managed.

—John Milton, from *Paradise Lost*

Contents

Introduction

Introduction

Adolescence is such a vulnerable time, when youngsters are facing so many changes. It is a time of growing pains and is especially challenging to a child's self-esteem. After all, their bodies are developing, and they are becoming more sensitive about their achievements in school and their social relationships. These challenges to a positive self-image usually peak in early adolescence, making this a crucial time for you as a parent to help your child establish a strong foothold on feeling good and adjusting with a positive self-image.

This book deals with raising a child's self-esteem during the stage of adolescence because doing so is fundamental to your child's healthy development. Self-esteem is based on fostering positive values and behaviors in your child. As a result, in this book, we cover a series of positive traits and values that lead to high self-esteem and ways that you as a parent can help facilitate them in your youngster. For example, how do you help your child become more confident or instill responsibility in him or her? In this book, you'll find ways to do that, complete with guidelines for conversations you can have with your child, teachable moments you can identify, and activities you can do to help build your child's positive self-image and enhance the values and behaviors you're trying to develop.

As you read this book, here are eight general themes and tips that apply to all the chapters.

1. When talking to your child about any of these 31 Things, start with an impersonal example or phrase, since adolescents can rebel or become defensive when they feel adults are lecturing them. For example, say, "I read an article (or saw a report on TV or a site on the Internet) that said young people today are . . . (fill in the issue)." Make the question open-

ended by then asking, "How do you feel about that?" instead of asking a question like "Do you agree?" that would get a "yes" or "no" answer that stops the conversation.

2. Each chapter ends with a lesson that serves as training for the mind. Like a mantra, each is a phrase that can be repeated to "fix" the desirable behavior or attitude into your child's mind. Have him repeat it, and repeat it often yourself, so it stays in your mind. Say it aloud to anchor it.

3. Some exercises are applicable to many chapters but are not repeated in the text. For example, positive self-talk helps in dealing with many issues. Look at the exercises in each chapter and see how they can apply to issues discussed in other chapters.

4. Some chapters have "teachable moments" to show how you can take advantage of a situation to teach your child a valuable lesson. A teachable moment

might involve explaining the consequences of a particular behavior. Or it could encourage you to discuss emotional reasons for a behavior. Adolescents are at a stage where their cognitive development allows for this kind of deeper understanding of dynamics, needs, feelings, and fears.

5. Some chapters also contain the section "modeling" to show how you can be a good role model for your child. Adolescents need a good role model—which you can be as a parent. That means you must practice the behavior you expect of your child. In other words, the rule is, "Do what I do," not "Do what I say, not what I do." Adolescents notice what their parents do and will either copy the behavior or do the opposite. Be sure you are practicing what you preach. Social modeling is a proven psychological principle: people (especially children) tend to copy what they see others around them do. If you've ever watched ducklings follow in their mother's footsteps, you know how this kind of developmental modeling works!

6. Some chapters have a section called "What triggers you?" This section encourages you to examine your own feelings and behaviors about that particular issue. For example, when it comes to perseverance, are you able to focus and finish (the lesson for that chapter's "Thing")? Explore your own deeper issues: What has happened in your childhood or past experience relative to that issue? Your adolescent's problem may trigger memories of your own youth when you had a similar problem, so you may become more anxious to face your child's issue. Or you may be having that same problem now. Confront and deal with your own problem so you do not push your child away. Check your own self-esteem level. If you need to feel more loved to raise your own self-esteem, have deeper fears that need to be dissolved, or need more positive attention, get those needs met or issues resolved. One good exercise: "Re-parent" yourself by picturing yourself being both the child and the parent giving you the attention you need.

7. Be an "askable parent": That means give your child the message that you are always there to be a helping hand. Even if you don't know an answer, you will try to find it out.

8. Many issues in these chapters are closely related, such as "Being responsible" and "Being on time." Go back and forth in the chapters, on your own and with your child, to see how all the issues come together.

Be involved in your child's life! Preteens and young teens need their parents—more than they would admit—although they may want you present under different terms and conditions than they previously did. Some parents misread the signals that their children send and back off too soon. For example, about 75 percent of American parents report high or moderate involvement in their nine-year-olds' school-related activities, but when children reach fourteen, the rate of parental involvement drops to 55 percent. The rate continues to drop throughout high school. But research shows that adolescents do better in school when their parents are involved in their lives, and that education works best when teachers and parents work closely with one another.

Your child's adolescence is a time of challenge and growth for both of you. As you read these chapters, it is our hope that you will begin to feel more in control of these changes and better able to deal with them, creating a happier life for the whole family.

The 31 Things

— 1 —

Sticking to it

— 1 —

Sticking to it

Perseverance means sticking to a task until it's complete. You know how adolescents can lose interest, get distracted or discouraged, or become frustrated, so they leave their homework incomplete, their room only partially clean, or their household task half done. You also know that success requires persistence and completion.

Popular culture causes distraction, with too many stimuli, such as scenes changing too quickly in TV shows and too many Internet sites to visit. This is all the more reason for parents to teach their children to focus on tasks until they are done. As the popular phrase goes, don't put off until tomorrow what you can do today.

Teachable moments

1. Explain the value of perseverance: finishing a task, pushing through obstacles and dealing with frustration, or eliminating whatever is stopping the flow, is key to success.

2. To train the behavior, stay with your child during the process of a task (cleaning her room, doing a homework assignment) to track the process of perseverance. For example, if your child is doing homework and suddenly gets up from the desk and turns on the TV, or switches from homework on the computer to a video game site, here's what to do: instead of criticizing or scolding (saying, "Get back to your homework," "I'm angry with you," or "You know you have to do your homework"), gently say something to acknowledge the distracting behavior ("That looks like a good thing to do after you finish your homework assignment"); be encouraging and reassuring ("That task is a challenge, but I know you

can do it," or "Some kids at your age get worried if they can actually complete the assignment or finish the math problem, and it can be scary!").

3. Be a cheerleader along the way, especially if they've gotten distracted. For example, if your child is writing about the presidents in American history, redirect her attention and help make it a fun and compelling task—e.g., ask a provocative question like, "What was the most interesting thing that you're learning that a president did?" Point out the value of focusing and finishing ("It feels so good when you see a task to the end").

4. Reward sticking to the task and also completing it. When your child starts the task, gets back to it after being distracted, or finishes, say, "That's wonderful!" "You did it: focus and finish!"

Modeling

Do you finish what you start? Are you always carrying over your to-do list to the next day? Set a good example and point out the behavior to your child. For example, have your child present when you wash the car and point out how you polish the hubcaps to finish the job. Make sure he's around when you're sending Christmas cards and show how you went through the whole list. When finished, say, "I feel great that I persevered through this task and finished it!"

Get to deeper issues

What is stopping your child from finishing? Is she afraid she won't do well or will be criticized? For example, your daughter might not finish her math homework because she feels she's not good at math or because she heard that girls can't do math. Ask, "How do you feel about doing math?"

"Do you think girls can be good at math?" Getting to the root of anxiety about personal success or an erroneous belief can release fear and re-instill confidence. You'll be surprised how acknowledging underlying fear, insecurity, or anxiety will help your child get back to the task.

Lesson: Focus and finish.

~ 2 ~

Building confidence

– 2 –

Building confidence

Confidence means knowing you are a worthwhile person. Kids learn to be confident by how they are treated in their families: if they are encouraged to speak up and to do things, they come to discover that they are capable. Kids at this age commonly feel gawky and awkward about their physical skills and emotions. They may be afraid to play basketball because they are afraid they can't make the basket, or not write for the school paper because they fear they aren't a good writer. Confidence is key to self-esteem, both personal confidence ("I can do this") and social confidence ("Others like being with me").

According to the U.S. Department of Education, youth often feel inadequate as they are trying to adapt to their changing bodies and relationships with friends and family. Young teens with low self-confidence can be lonely, awkward with others, sensitive to criticism, and less likely to join activities and form friendships. This isolates them further and slows their ability to develop a better self-image. Saddled with low self-confidence, when they do make friends, they are more vulnerable to peer pressure. Adolescents who lack confidence may hold back in class or do the opposite—act out to gain attention. At worst, a lack of confidence usually leads to self-destructive behavior and habits—smoking or drug or alcohol use, sexual behavior, or even self-injury.

Teachable moments

Every time your child does something that makes him feel good about himself, make a big deal about it. Say, "That is so terrific! I am so glad you could do that!" Do this even over small things and be very specific. If your daughter combs her hair perfectly every morning, say, "I am so proud that you take such good care of yourself every morning and that I never have to remind you." If your son puts the top back on the chocolate milk, say, "You're so good about being responsible in putting the cap back on the chocolate milk."

Be very complimentary and supportive. Express care by saying, "I'm glad to see you," "I love you so much," "I'm glad you are my child," or "You can do anything if you want to." If your child is giving a speech at school, have her practice in front of you and point out all the things she is doing right instead of what is not up to par. That approach of emphasizing the positive builds confidence.

Lesson: Yes, I can!

~ 3 ~

Listening

– 3 –

Listening

A dolescents are at a stage where they are developing more sophisticated verbal communication skills, so this is an important time to help them learn how to be good listeners. Being a good listener is important to self-esteem because it helps connect you to people and makes others find you likeable.

Teachable moment

The best communicators do what is called "active listening." Teach your child how to listen actively by following these guidelines:

What not to do: Don't interrupt, talk over people, and change the subject when the other person is talking. The worst thing a child can do when a friend says something such as, "I was upset today in school because the teacher wasn't pleased with my homework and said something nasty to me," is to interrupt by saying he had the same experience, and to go on to talk about himself, changing the focus from his friend to himself and cutting the friend off.

What to do: Listen carefully to what someone is saying, put yourself in their shoes, feel what they may be feeling, and ask questions to help them express further what they are trying to say. Instead of your child interrupting to talk about himself, as in the previous example, he should empathize with his friend's feelings by saying, "That must have felt bad," or ask a question like, "How did that make you feel?" That way, his friend feels he cares about what he is saying.

Lesson: I am a good listener.

— 4 —

Making smart decisions

– 4 –

Making smart decisions

A dolescence is a crucial time to learn smart decision-making, since this age group will be facing many peer pressures and needs to know how to make wise choices and resist being pushed into doing what would not be in their best interest.

Smart decision-making involves problem solving—recognizing a problem or opportunity, and finding a solution while considering possible consequences of choices.

Parents know the value of decision-making when they offer choices to their children, even toddler-aged children. For example, mothers may ask, "Would you like to have your dinner now or in a half hour?" They also train children to know the consequences of their choices; for example, "If you don't clean up your room, we won't be able to go to the park this afternoon like you wanted to do."

Decision-making becomes more intense in adolescence when dealing with making friendships, increased pressure to do well in school, and peer pressure about things like drugs and sex. A greater ability to make choices and see consequences starts at eight years old, when cognitive development allows them to understand shades of gray instead of just black and white.

Caution

If your child tends to say "no" a lot at this age, do not be alarmed since this can reflect a desire to feel independent rather than reflecting rebellion. The phase can pass.

Exercise

Choose three particular problems that your child is facing and explore the options for what to do and the consequences of each choice, according to this chart. Ask your child to fill in the answers to the choice and consequence sections.

	PROBLEM	CHOICE (what to do)	CONSEQUENCE
1			
2			
3			

Then ask your child to answer these questions:

What choice my parents would like me to make:

What choice I would like to make:

Lesson: I can make smart choices.

— 5 —

From shy to assertive

— 5 —

From shy to assertive

Many adolescents suffer from being painfully shy. Shyness can be charming and show respect and reserve in a child. It can also be a common reaction to being unsure about how to behave when going through the normal stages of social development. Almost everyone has experienced shyness at some point in life, and even public figures and celebrities like Michael Jackson and Barbara Walters have admitted to being shy. But when your child coils back from people, won't go out or socialize, or won't speak up in class because of feeling too shy, it's a problem.

The tendency to be shy can be due to many factors: genetics (some babies are born with "stranger anxiety"), chemical imbalances, culture, learned behavior (by parents' example or warning: "Don't try that," "Wait until you're spoken to"), a reaction to others being too extraverted, or the result of experiences (e.g., being rejected). Researchers estimate that about 10 percent of people are born shy because of brain chemistry (amounts of monoamine oxidase, serotonin, and cortisol). Whatever the reason, your child can learn to be more outgoing.

Caution

Accept your child's trait and do not push her into being a social butterfly or Miss Personality when it doesn't suit her, just because doing so would make you feel better.

Teachable moments

1. Reassure your child that everyone can feel shy, but it is healthy to feel free to speak up and choose to mix with people. Explore deeper reasons for

shyness, as described above. Ask, "What are you afraid will happen if you ask for what you want?" They may fear that they will owe someone back who gives them something they want.

2. Help your child understand why others are shy. For example, at this age, girls and boys are sensitive about whether others talk to them, or tease them. Girls often ask, "Why do guys act like they don't like you, or they don't have anything to say to you, when you're sure they do?" The answer is they could just be too shy, inexperienced, or socially scared to be up front about their interest. They may not know what to say, what to do if she responds, or even how to handle being teased by their male friends about talking to girls. In the old days, boys used to pull girls' pigtails in class and the girl would think he hated her, but really it was his awkward way of showing her attention. The lesson for this teachable moment: your child should be more direct if he likes someone and not pretend otherwise.

3. Use the "Reinforcement Rule": reward what you want repeated. For example, whenever your child is not being shy but being outgoing in a positive way, say, "Oh, that is great, I love when you're so outgoing. Don't you feel good about that? How does that feel for you?"

Exercise

To help your child become more assertive, have her practice the yes/no exercise. Ask your child to make a list of three things that she would really like to say "yes" to but has been afraid to. For example, "Yes, I would like you to help me with my math homework," " Yes, I really want you to coach me more on my soccer skills," or "Yes, I really want to go shopping and buy that dress I liked." The second part is to ask her to say "no" to three things she wishes she could say "no" to but is afraid to, such as "No, I will not clean my room today," "No, I don't want to invite Mary to sleep over," or "No, I don't want to give away that shirt that is too small on me."

In the second version of the yes/no exercise, your child says "yes" and sees how loudly she can say it. Then she says "no" as loudly as she can say it. Which one comes more easily? Whichever one she said more softly she should practice saying as loudly as the other.

Lesson: I can say "yes" or "no."

− 6 −

Setting boundaries

– 6 –

Setting boundaries

People have psychological boundaries just like countries have borders that cannot be crossed without permission. Setting boundaries is important at this age to establish a safety zone so no one can take advantage of them or be abusive.

Psychological boundaries exist on three different levels: (1) soft, in which people merge easily with others and can be easily manipulated; (2) rigid, in which a person is walled off so nobody can get close physically or emotionally (this often happens after a bad experience or physical, emotional, or psychological abuse); and (3) reflexible, which is in between soft and rigid. Spongy boundaries can at first make the child feel unsure about what to let in and what to keep out. But ultimately, having flexible boundaries is most ideal for allowing the child to select who or what to let close or keep out. Therefore, your child cannot be easily manipulated or exploited. The goal is to be wisely selective, depending on the appropriate time, place, or circumstance.

A quiz to test boundaries

Have your child take this quiz: rate how often the below apply on a scale of 0 to 10, where 0 means "never" and 10 means "very often."

Q: How often do you feel others make you do something you do not want to do?
Q: How often are you afraid to tell others that you don't want to do something?

If the answer is over 5 to these two questions, then it's important to help your child focus on setting stricter boundaries.

Q: How often do you feel you shut people out?
Q: How often do you feel that you purposely don't let people know how you feel or get close to you but regret it?

If the answer is over 5 to these two questions, then it's crucial to focus on helping your child have more flexible boundaries.

Exercises

To develop stricter boundaries:
1. Practice saying, "No, you can't," "No, I won't," or "No, you can't do that to me," and just plain "Stop!" Those are words for your child to use when she feels people are doing things that are invasive or abusive.

2. Physicalize a "safe space": Have your child demonstrate a space around him that is his "safe space," sweeping his arms around and moving steps forward

or sideways to show how close people are allowed to get. Research on what's called "personal distance" shows that this proportion differs according to culture; for example, British people tend to stand farther apart from each other and touch less than those from Latin countries.

3. As mentioned in other chapters in this book, enrolling your child in a martial arts class is a great way for him to learn to set boundaries and experience the power of his own body and spirit to control how others treat him, and to protect himself from other's assaults.

To help develop more flexible boundaries:
1. Ask your child what he or she is afraid for people to know about. Discuss and ease those fears.

2. As previously noted, physicalize being more open, this time asking your child to stretch out his or her arms and feel what it is like to be more "open."

Teachable moments

Describe to your child that people should not take advantage of her, abuse her, or force her to do something she doesn't want to do. This is especially important when it comes to sex and drugs, that children should not give in to peer pressure, and girls should not accede to sex with boys and let their boundaries be crossed. Encourage your child that she is able to set her limits about what she will accept—or not accept—from others. But also emphasize that allowing others to get close to her can be rewarding and provides the basis for intimacy and love.

Lesson: Stop or go! I can let you in or keep you out of my territory.

~ 7 ~

Being kind

~ 7 ~

Being kind

Of course you teach your child good manners, but at this stage of development, adolescents can be awkward about saying nice things to others. So even if they don't intend to be mean, they can say things that come across as disrespectful or unkind.

Adolescence is a good stage of development to instill the value of kindness and doing nice things for others. As Mother Teresa said, "Kindness is a language we all understand. Even the blind can see it and the deaf can hear it."

Teachable moment

Doing good has been proven to stimulate chemicals in the body that make you and others feel good.

When your child does something kind, or when someone else does something nice for another person, point it out to your child. Tell your child that doing one kind act a day will make him—and the other person and everyone around—happier and healthier.

Exercises

1. Ask your child to go with you to volunteer for some organization that serves others; for example, to serve holiday dinner to the needy. Pick a volunteer organization that has some meaning to your child and family. For example, if Aunt Sue has cancer, then volunteering for the local hospital to bring toys to children hospitalized with cancer is meaningful.

2. If your child says something that you find sounds nasty, then say, "I know you didn't mean for that to come out that way, but how you said it sounded

unpleasant to me. Is there any other way you can say that in a kinder way?"

3. Model simple acts of kindness. Ask your child, "In what ways can you be kind to others?" "What do you think would bring a bright light into someone's life who isn't happy right now?" For example, ask, "Why don't you take a carton of milk over to Mrs. Smith who just broke her hip?" "Can you help your friend with French homework since you are so good at languages?" "Will you help your little brother clean his room?" Encourage kids to gather together the toys or clothes they no longer need to give to someone less fortunate who could use them.

Lesson: Do one little act of kindness every day.

~ 8 ~

Being on time

– 8 –

Being on time

Being on time is being able to complete a required task or fulfill an obligation at a previously designated time. Being punctual is important because it shows that you can be trusted and that others can rely on you. As a parent, you know how important it is to be on time, and you also know as an adult how annoying it is when people say they are going to do one thing—such as meet you at a particular time—and then don't do it. Understandably, you get angry (after all, your time is valuable) and start mistrusting the other person. If the person is chronically late, a bad cycle gets set up in which you come late in anticipation of their being late, which is not your style. Your adolescent needs to know that people's time is valuable and that in later life, especially in business, people will not accept late behavior.

Teachable moments

1. When your child says, "Oh, Mommy, come watch me throw my ball," reply, "I'm washing the dishes right at this second, and I'll be with you in thirty minutes." Then make sure you keep that appointment. Make sure that whatever you are doing, you are outside in exactly thirty minutes in the yard tossing the ball with your child. Then state very clearly, "See, I told you I would be here in thirty minutes, and I am proud of myself that I absolutely kept my word." Pointing it out is very important to make a clear lesson that you followed through at the agreed-upon time you promised.

2. Discuss lateness with your child. That includes talking about why people are late—on the simplest level, it can be a lack of organization, but on a deep-

er level, it can reflect feeling anxiety or fear about meeting up with that person or doing whatever was planned. Rock stars may keep their audiences waiting, and your child may think that is acceptable, but explain that this can also be "diva" behavior or even fear of performing on stage! Understanding lateness also includes discussing how people are affected in negative ways when someone is late: they get angry at or distrustful of that person, and disinterested in continuing to make plans with him. Being late also tends to signify "I'm more important," which insults the other person.

Unexpected things can always come up to make us late, such as an urgent e-mail or traffic. But it is important to emphasize to your child that there are no excuses!

Exercises

1. Ask, "What do you gain of out of being late? How does this help you?" This may sound strange when a

behavior has negative consequences, but psychologically, there is always a gain even in such cases. For example, your child might say, "If I come late, then I know I'm not the one waiting and being angry."

2. Ask what the positive outcomes are of being on time. Being on time makes you feel good about yourself, and allows other people to trust you. Also, what are the negative consequences of not being on time? Other people are going to lose respect for you and will not keep their agreements with you. If you're late, people may not trust you or believe you in other situations and will stop making plans with you. They'll also feel bad about themselves, as if they don't matter enough to you.

Modeling

Set a good example by being on time yourself. Keep all your time commitments to your child. Make a deliberate effort to pick him up from school at 2:30 P.M., be there on time, and point to your watch and say, "I am proud that I promised you I would be here at 2:30 P.M. and made it." You can add how difficult it was as an example of how other things can come up, but that you still organized yourself to make it with no excuses. Say, "It was tough to be on time because I had a last-minute call that took time, but I told the person on the phone that I had to meet you on time, so I got off the phone and rescheduled to finish that conversation." This shows that you honor your child's time, and that you made plans around what was an important commitment to each other.

Lesson: There are no excuses for being late: as the saying goes, "be there or be square."

– 9 –

Learning patience

— 9 —

Learning patience

Adolescents are impulsive. They want immediate gratification: they want what they want when they want it. Instead, they need to learn what's called "delayed gratification," which means that it can take time before getting what you want. In other words, they have to learn patience.

Patience requires what's called "frustration tolerance," which means learning how not to become irritable, angry, or aggressive when you are not satisfied right away.

This lesson is a hard one in this day and age, since contemporary culture is built on immediate gratification, evident in fast food, fast-paced video games, and instant messaging. People don't even have to wait in line for movie tickets—they can click online to purchase them before getting to the theater or use a kiosk in the lobby.

Teachable moments

1. Give some examples of good things that take time. For example, it took nine months for your child to grow in your body until he or she was born. It also takes time for close friendships to grow, as you spend more time and do more things together.

2. Elaborate on the payoffs for waiting. Be reassuring that results can come in due time. Describe how throughout life people may not "hop" when you want them to, or events may not occur in timing to your liking.

Exercises

1. Engage your child in an activity that requires waiting. For example, plant a seed for a vegetable

or flower that obviously takes time to grow and blossom.

2. Look at a wristwatch and ask your child to sit quietly for a minute to get the sense of time, to feel how long a minute actually is, and to be patient while waiting for the minute to go by.

3. Give your child some techniques to deal with frustration while waiting. Use the time to accomplish something else. For example, while on hold on the phone, look up something on the Internet. Another technique: breathe deeply to calm down.

Lesson: Patience is a virtue.

— 10 —

Turning body hate into body love

– 10 –

Turning body hate into body love

Adolescence is a very vulnerable time when it concerns body image since young bodies are in the process of change as part of normal development. But kids compare themselves to friends, more often coming up short (in height—or in all other attributes!). They worry about being the shortest or tallest in class, that their teeth are more crooked, or that they wear glasses. Young girls cry about their breast size, and boys fret that other boys have more facial hair.

Studies show that over eight out of ten people despise something about their appearance. Therefore, adolescence is an important time to help young people accept how they look so they can develop body confidence throughout their lives.

Teachable moments

1. Change self-talk. Encourage adolescents to change their thinking from loving their bodies only from the outside, thinking, "If I look good (thin or buff enough), then I can feel okay," or "If I'm not perfect from the outside, then I hate my body and myself," to developing a healthier mindset: loving their bodies from the inside. Tell them to feel good about who they are instead of how they look. There's truth to the saying that beauty comes from within.

2. Explain that everyone looks different: no two noses, faces, or body shapes are exactly alike. Help your child appreciate her differences and uniqueness.

3. Be reassuring: explain that kids develop at different stages and levels in terms of height, weight, and other body parts. Some girls develop breasts and menstruate earlier than others; some boys' voices get

deeper, or facial or pubic hair grows faster or thicker than that of other boys. These are normal differences.

4. Emphasize to your child that most kids go through a stage of being critical about their bodies—consider it part of growing pains! Even celebrities are critical of their bodies. What seems like an undesirable characteristic now can turn into something attractive. For example, actress Kim Basinger and rock star Steven Tyler hated their big lips, but for both of them, that attribute ended up being part of their attraction.

5. Help your child love his body: it's an incredible, magnificent creation that does miracles 24/7, whether sitting, walking, or playing.

Exercises

1. Have your child think of her body as a friend. Would she say to a friend, "You're ugly?" Explain to her to be as kind as she would to someone she cares about.

2. Mirror exercise: tell your adolescent to look in the mirror and notice what he likes instead of what he doesn't like, and say it out loud: "I have beautiful eyes," "My hair is so silky," or "My arms are so strong."

3. Shift focus and self-talk. Encourage them to shift their attention from a physical inadequacy (or what they believe to be an inadequacy) to some other quality they have that they can feel good about. For example: "Maybe I'm shorter than others, but I'm intelligent."

4. Review what is reasonable to change. Frizzy hair can easily be fixed with a hair iron that can be purchased at any drugstore for a reasonable price.

Caution

Don't let the pursuit of changes go too far. Reassure your child that some physical attributes will naturally change as he or she gets older (getting taller, breasts getting larger, hair getting thicker) and that they can also change some things, such as eating habits and weight. But beware of drastic changes that adolescents want to make too early. Too many kids at too young of an age look at magazines that show "perfect bodies" (photoshopped anyway to remove imperfections) and begin thinking about plastic surgery. Discourage that!

Modeling

Concerning appearances, it's natural if you as a parent feel anxious about who you consider "bad" role models in the media; for example, you may think superstar Miley Cyrus—a hugely popular role model for preteens—is growing up too quickly, dressing too sexy, and acting way too mature for her age. Recognize your own attitudes. Instead of criticizing these teen idols, be a good role model by asking what your child thinks about them. Getting your child to explore her own attitudes is key to growing up. Also, recognize whether you are too critical of your own body. Catch yourself before your child overhears you complaining, "I look so fat in this dress," "Look at all these horrible wrinkles," or "I hate my hair."

Another aspect of body love: good personal hygiene

Adolescents can get lax about daily practices associated with good health, which helps them love their bodies. This daily routine includes flossing teeth, brushing hair, showering, and cleaning under nails. Your adolescent may be lazy or just may not be aware of the importance of these routines for present and future health and for social acceptability.

Exercise

Go to the convenience store or discount department store together and pick out products needed for good body hygiene. Have your child select among the different varieties of soap, shampoo, toothbrushes and toothpaste, mouthwash, antiperspirant, tissues, nail files, skin cleansers, and even toilet paper. Include getting cotton swabs to clean out their ears.

Teachable moments

1. Emphasize that good personal hygiene is important for social reasons (to be presentable to others) and also for general good health. Explain the importance of taking care of your body for feeling good and also for looking your best. That means brushing your teeth (and flossing) and washing your face every morning and night. Routines are important to start in adolescence, not just to obtain the type that beauty magazines promote, but for personal health and well-being. Boys need to know this even more than girls; for example, tell your son it's not unmanly to use a skin cream. Routines don't have to cost lots of money: home manicure kits can be just

as effective as going to a beauty parlor. But you can also treat your child to a trip to the beauty parlor for something special, to learn about good grooming and also for you and her to bond.

2. You can also use fun history facts to help your child maintain good hygiene. Adolescents learn in history class about the famous Roman baths (inexpensive, so everyone would be clean!), but here are some more fun facts to share with your child.

Soap was invented in 2800 B.C. in ancient Mesopotamia, made by boiling animal fats or vegetable oils with ashes—which would have been pretty harsh and abrasive. The Greeks and Romans preferred oiling their bodies, then scraping them clean with a strigil, a curved piece of wood.

In contrast, deodorant is a modern invention. Before the late 1800s, people just covered up body odor with perfume. Ancient Egyptians, for example, applied scented oil to their underarms and shaved their hair and wore wigs on top of which they set a perfume-filled wax cone that would melt during the day to release the scent.

Likewise, roll toilet paper wasn't invented until the nineteenth century; before that, people used leaves, moss, corn cobs (really!), scraps of cloth, sponges on a stick, or—ew!—their left hand (especially in the dry Middle East where leaves are scarce—which is why that hand is still never used for shaking hands or eating).

For dental care, ancient people used a stick with a frayed end covered with rubbed ashes; pumice or ground shells mixed with herbs; and wine or urine as mouthwash. Later, ground eggshells or borax powder was used as a cleaning abrasive. For menstruation, women used rolled-up cloth or cotton, strips of animal pelt, moss, or sponges. Pre-manufactured cloth pads were available in the mid-nineteenth century, generally held on by some sort of belt.

Lesson: I take care of my body.

~ 11 ~

Overcoming guilt

− 11 −

Overcoming guilt

Guilt is a feeling that occurs when you believe you have thought, said, or done something you regret, or didn't do something you thought you should have, that ended up making you feel like a bad person and may have also hurt someone else.

In Freud's theory of guilt, if the id takes over and unleashes an unbridled urge, the superego, a form of conscience, becomes critical.

The law insists that everyone is innocent until proven guilty. But in real-life interpersonal relations, you can torture yourself imagining wrong done to others and punishment due to the offenders, or others can unfairly accuse you of harm, causing you to have a guilty conscience.

Adolescents, especially those who are people pleasers but who have once been "caught in the act" (however small, like stealing cookies from the cookie jar), can feel guilty even when they have not done anything wrong. In other words, they may shiver if the principal or a police officer walks by, immediately imagining they have done something wrong.

What triggers you?

Are you guilt-inducing? Guilt can be induced in a subtle manner or in an overt manner. An example of inducing guilt is a mother staying up late waiting for her daughter to come home from a chaperoned party then moaning, "You made me stay up so late worrying about you. How can you be so thoughtless?" Guilt is stimulated by emphasizing how the child's behavior made the mother suffer.

Parents who induce guilt may be trying to manipulate their child, control their child's behavior, or make the child feel sorry for them. It is unhealthy to use your child for your own needs.

If you punish your child too harshly for eating sweets before dinner, she might resent you and eventually feel rebellious. She might even sneak behind your back and purposely eat candy before dinner at other people's houses, just to rebel and get even with you. In other words, by being too critical, you may not instill any lasting positive behavior change, improvement, or alteration in her urges.

Exercises for you to deal with your own guilt

1. Imagine a transgression and imagine putting yourself on trial for it. Argue both sides. Purposely play out the actions as if you were exonerated on all counts.

2. Trace the source of your guilt. Such feelings can be engendered by religious traditions that make people feel guilty for their actions and thoughts,

which must be punished, confessed, or excused by performing certain rituals.

3. If you feel guilty, get to the bottom of the feeling. Is it helping you to be sympathetic to another person? Do you prefer to blame yourself than face what would happen if you accuse someone else?

4. What could you be doing to contribute to your child's unwarranted problem with guilt? In actuality, no one makes anyone feel something, but you may be facilitating insecurity. Like the aforementioned example, you could be fostering insecurity and inducing guilt if your child comes home late from playing with a friend and you scream, "How could you do this to me? You ruined my whole plans. I was supposed to go to my friend's house and then pick up some things at the store for my cold. Now I may be sicker than ever because I can't go." Ask yourself: What's the value of imposing all this on my child? You've upset your child, yourself, and

your relationship by scolding your child and causing your own indigestion.

5. Focus on what is in the best interest of your child by what you say, and respond accordingly. Don't put guilt trips on your child because of your own problems. Think of your child's problem first before you start making demands on him for making you feel bad, or for what you are supposed to take care of yourself.

Exercises to help your child deal with guilt

1. Ask your child to repeat what he feels guilty about towards you, and talk it through so you can convincingly offer forgiveness, or clarify that you were not as upset as he thought about what happened.

2. Encourage him to excuse himself. Guide him to say: I don't intend to hurt my parents, so I don't have to torture myself thinking I am a bad person.

3. Teach your child to learn from guilt. Explain: If you feel you made a mistake, become more mindful and aware of your behavior and resolve to do something different next time.

Teachable moments

If your child is struggling with unnecessary guilt, say, "You're never a 'bad' person, you just may do things that others disapprove of or don't agree with." Continue by saying, "Let's review what you feel guilty about and see whether there's anything you can do to make the situation better."

Lesson: I can free myself from guilt.

– 12 –

Taming the green-eyed monster

– 12 –

Taming the green-eyed monster

The green-eyed monster—jealousy—particularly surfaces at this tender age when adolescents are becoming self-conscious about their identity and attributes and start comparing themselves to others, being vulnerable to thinking someone is better than they are.

Jealousy consumes self-esteem, sabotages confidence, and drives away friends. Your child is jealous if he or she is always pointing out how others are better, complaining that others have more, or persistently saying things like, "All the girls are prettier than me," or "All the boys play better than me."

Teachable moments

1. Emphasize that all children are different and special in their own way, and that no one quality is

better or worse than another.

2. Turn painful jealousy into positive self-improvement. Notice what your child envies in others (being popular, acting cool, being good at sports) and help your child develop those positive attributes as much as you can. The secret here is that what kids admire in others is often what they really want for themselves.

3. Tell your child to redirect energy: reinforce the message that the minute your child feels jealous about another child, he should focus instead on what's wonderful about himself.

4. Teach a positive "life philosophy" about abundance: others having more does not mean you have less. Instead, the more your friends have or do, the more is possible for you to have or do.

5. The grass is not always greener; everyone's garden has patches of brown. Teach your child that

even if a friend has better grades in English than she does, she may want your help with History.

6. Explain the cycle of jealousy: a jealous child may be surrounded by others who are equally jealous of him. Encourage your child to select friends who celebrate his success instead of competing with him or being begrudging. Teach your child that being happy for others' success makes their own world a better place by being surrounded by goodness.

7. Reassure your child about what is special about him or her. Constantly point out specific attributes ("You draw so well") and generally being special ("You are so special to me").

What triggers you?

Look into yourself: examine your own Envy Meter. Are you jealous of others? Catch yourself before saying things like, "Your friend's mother always wears beautiful clothing, I wish we could afford that." Make sure you are not stimulating jealousy by comparing one child to another (saying, "Your sister is always well behaved," or "Why don't you get good grades like your brother?").

Exercise

Turn envy into appreciation and self-improvement: ask your child, "What quality do you like about Bobby?" then explore how it's a wonderful attribute and ask, "How can you be more like that to feel good about yourself?" or, "Instead of being jealous about a friend, how can you develop those good qualities?"

Lesson: What you envy in others, develop in yourself.

~ 13 ~

Stop bullying

~ 13 ~

Stop bullying

A bully is someone who either alone or in a group repeatedly picks on or tries to harm another person, physically or psychologically, who seems defenseless or weaker. Direct attacks include hitting, name calling, teasing, or taunting, and indirect attacks include spreading rumors or trying to make others reject the victim. According to a 2008 national survey of students in grades six through ten, *Bullying Behaviors Among U.S. Youth,* almost 30 percent of youth (or over 5.7 million) in the United States are either a bully, a target of bullying, or both. Specifically, the National Youth Violence Prevention Resource Center found that 13 percent reported bullying others, 11 percent reported being the target of bullies, and another 6 percent said that they bullied others and were bullied themselves. Bullying occurs in real life and also on the Internet, with tragic consequences. For example, one case reported that a teen committed suicide because of being taunted by peers on Internet sites as being homosexual.

Being bullied means your child feels picked on and is being terrorized by another person or a group trying purposely to hurt him or her emotionally or physically. Your child might be being hit, called names, teased or taunted, ganged up on, or had mean rumors spread about him or her. As the survey statistics from *Bullying Behaviors Among U.S. Youth* note, more than one in ten adolescents ages twelve through fifteen reported being bullied, and 160,000 kids stay home every day because they fear bullies.

What you can do if your child is a bully

1. Understand why children bully. A bully usually feels powerless inside and overcompensates by dominating others. If your child is feeling frightened

deep down, examine what might be making him or her feel so insecure. Bullies are angry: address what is making your child so angry. Bullying can also be circular: a child who intentionally hurts others might be hurt by others, essentially doing to others what is done to him. In psychological terms this is called "identifying with the aggressor." Examine whether someone is mistreating your bully child, being overly critical, or physically beating or abusing him. Stopping this can interrupt the cycle. Is your child repeating patterns he or she saw in the household? Maybe the mother is being mistreated by the father, or a parent is always belittling a sibling.

2. Step in and stop it. Refuse to allow your child to continue hurting another. Don't be afraid to discipline. Tell them that their behavior is unacceptable (but criticize the behavior, not the child). Then explore with your child why he or she is being a bully. Ask questions like, "What are you so angry about?" and "Who has ever hurt you?" Also ask if he sees

anything at home that reminds him of hurting others, and promise that you will do something to stop that from happening too.

What you can do if your child is bullied

1. Acknowledge that the experience, and resulting sad or terrified feelings, are real. Say, "I believe you. I know that hurts." Don't think your child is being oversensitive or is exaggerating.

2. Reassure your child that action can be taken to stop the behavior. Say you believe him or her and that you will do something if needed.

3. Tell your child that being bullied doesn't mean he or she is bad, weak, or inferior.

4. Help them practice self-talk and saying no: "I will not be abused;" "I deserve to be treated with respect."

5. Enroll them in martial arts classes to develop personal power.

Teachable moment

Teach your child that bullying is unacceptable but to understand why bullies behave that way—not to excuse the behavior, but for your child to feel more empowered. Explain that some kids do bad things, like bullying, because of their own insecurity and maybe how they are badly treated by others.

Caution

Never blame your child for being bullied, but do emphasize that there are some characteristics to develop that can prevent being victimized, like being more assertive.

What triggers you?

Monitor your own reaction. If you have ever been bullied or victimized in any way, you will empathize greatly with your child's predicament. Don't panic or overreact but do consider reasonable solutions. Empower your child to take action independently (avoid bullies, tell a bully to stop) before intervening (calling the bully's parents, seeing school authorities, calling police if appropriate).

Lesson: Bullies are weak, not strong. No one has the right to mistreat you. Remember the Golden Rule: Treat others as you would like to be treated yourself.

— 14 —

Feeling rejected by the in-crowd

― 14 ―

Feeling rejected by the in-crowd

Rejection is painful. Nobody likes to feel that others don't like them, that they don't "measure up," or that they're not "good enough." But everyone goes through those feelings at some point in their life. Adolescents are particularly sensitive to rejection since at this stage in life, they want desperately to be accepted by others, especially those they perceive to be the in-crowd.

Teachable moments

1. It's normal to want to be in the in-crowd. It's natural for your adolescent to even feel inconsolable when not accepted by who he thinks are the "cool" kids. Almost no rationalization or explanation helps

salve the hurt feelings. Only when he's much older can he truly feel that the in-crowd doesn't matter, that he can create his own crowd, that those who don't see his value are missing out and aren't worth caring about. Even though hearing these things won't stop the hurt, say them anyway, so he might get some quiet consolation by at least hearing the wisdom.

2. Explain the normal reactions to feeling rejected: hurt, depression, anger, frustration, irritability. Also describe normal behavioral reactions, like losing your temper (yelling at a younger sibling for no reason), withdrawing (locking himself in his room), or rejecting someone else (doing to another what was done to him).

3. Tell your child that she shouldn't feel she's not good enough or obsess over how she can change to be accepted ("If only I were prettier . . .").

4. Explain that it's okay to feel sad, but then it's healthy to change your attention to doing something that makes you feel good.

5. Advise your adolescent to seek out friends who like him. Tell him not to fall prey to low self-image in which "I don't want to belong to a club who wants me as a member." Tell your child to join the club that wants him and to make new friends who make him feel good about himself.

Lesson: I go where I'm appreciated.

– 15 –

From jeers to cheers

~ 15 ~

From jeers to cheers

Kids know what it's like to be either jeered or cheered from being at sports events at school. It feels bad to be "booed" and great to have everyone clapping and jumping for joy at what you did. Some sports stars have admitted that they are motivated by booing, to prove the crowds are wrong and that they can perform. Frankly, this is a less healthy motivation for success than being bolstered by others' appreciation.

Most children are devastated, though, by disapproval from others. This is normal, as adolescents need others' approval to bolster feeling good about themselves. While ultimately the goal of this book is to help you help your child feel good inside without needing others' approval, it is healthy to encourage your child to seek out friends who cheer him or her rather than those who are critical or judgmental. It's challenging enough that at this age, kids become judgmental and critical of themselves and of others, resulting in their being hypersensitive to taunting or feeling not good enough.

As a parent, if you know your child is seeking out and hanging out with "ego busters," that's a sign that your child doesn't feel very good about herself (since friends mirror your self-image), and a signal for you to step in and help.

Teachable moment

Pick friends who boost, not bust, your ego.

Exercises

1. With your child, go through the list of their friends, and say, "Now tell me on a scale of zero to ten, with ten being the most and zero the least, how

good does (fill-in-the-name) make you feel about yourself?" The next question on the same zero-to-ten scale is, "How do you feel after you are with this person?" If the numbers are less than seven, then you and your child know these friends are "ego busters" instead of "ego boosters." Review all the friends who are ego boosters and ask, "What is it about (that friend) that makes you feel good?" Praise them for being with this friend and say, "I'm glad you're friends with him because that makes you feel good about yourself." Or say, "It's healthy for you to be with people who make you feel good because they are mirrors of how you feel about yourself."

2. Go to a sports event with your child and watch the cheering squad. Point out how your child can be a cheerleader to herself and also to her friends. How much she cheers friends on will extend to feelings about herself.

What triggers you?

How are you contributing? Do the same exercise for your own friends and associates. Using those same scales of zero to ten, are they "ego busters" or "'ego boosters"? If the former, then decide to change your choice of companions.

**Lesson: Two, four, six, eight,
whom do I appreciate? Me, me, me!**

– 16 –

Toning down drama queens

– 16 –

Toning down drama queens

Being emotional is normal, but over-the-top reactions are draining for your child and can paradoxically reveal a fear of experiencing real feelings. You'll know the line has been crossed if it feels like the house is falling down. For example, you ask your daughter to put the dishes in the sink and she screams, "I work myself to death but no one appreciates what I do in this house!" or she tells you her friends went to the mall without her and exclaims, "Everybody hates me and I have no friends!" Or she didn't get a good grade on a test and cries she'll never get into college and locks herself in her room, screaming and sobbing.

It's nice that in these situations your daughter is expressing feelings, but these reactions reveal exaggerated emotion for the situation. What's really going on: being a drama queen—or too emotional—means that the deeper feeling is really scary. Deep down these children feel fragile.

These adolescents need to learn how to modulate—not get rid of—strong emotions, and to experience feelings without getting frightened.

Exercise

Ask yourself these questions to help identify whether your child is overly emotional:

Q: Does she cry at the drop of a hat?

Q: Does she say often, "I don't think you really love me."

Q: Does she fly off the handle (for example, if you ask whether she had a good day at school)?

Q: Does she always seem to be helping or "saving" other children?

Q: Does she seem overly sensitive about any criticism or any sign of not being liked enough?

Q: Does the emotional reaction seem to you to be out of proportion to what actually happened?

Teachable moments

To help your child modulate emotions:
1. Help her focus on the facts of what happened instead of how she feels about it—not to get rid of feelings, but to balance them with reality. For example, if she says everyone hates her at school, ask, "What exactly did they say to make you feel that way? Tell me exactly what happened." Going over the facts will help her to see the situation more realistically and to accept real feelings. Then you can explore other interpretations or actions, such as, "What your friend did made you feel unwanted, but it doesn't have to mean that she hates you." It's also helpful—and okay—to explore ways to cope using

healthy rationalizations ("I have other friends," or "I am better off without her because I can look for friends who like me") rather than exaggerations ("I have no friends") or anticipating an awful future ("I'll never have friends").

2. Ask, "What's the absolute worst that can happen?" Interestingly, making the drama even more dramatic purges fears and allows for a calmer, more realistic approach.

Modeling

Is your own behavior irrational or too emotional? If your child doesn't do her homework, do you exaggerate the consequences, threatening that she will never get into college, or never find a husband? Did your child overhear you telling your husband, "If you're late one more time, I'm going to walk out this door and never see you again?" Check your emotions before you let loose, and purposely underreact. Since exaggerating emotions actually pushes away true feelings, tell your adolescent to have the courage to examine what you may be afraid to feel. In this way, you can be a healthy example for your child about how to deal with feelings.

Lesson: I can feel my real feelings instead of creating a stage character with "lights, camera, action."

~ 17 ~

Emerging from down in the dumps

― 17 ―

Emerging from down in the dumps

The statistics on the number of teens who are depressed are shocking. Studies show that one in five children have some sort of mental, behavioral, or emotional problem, and that one in ten may have a serious emotional problem. One in eight adolescents may suffer from depression. Yet less than a third receive any sort of intervention or treatment, with the majority struggling through pain when treatment could help. The consequences of untreated depression are dire: being depressed through adulthood, getting in trouble with the law, and worse, attempting suicide. Some suicides look like accidents, so the depression is not noticed.

A Brown University report noted that even parents who seem to have a good relationship with their young children do not recognize the symptoms of depression.

Suicide is the sixth leading cause of death among children ages five to fourteen. What's worse are the statistics on youth suicide. According to a Healthy-Place: American Mental Health Channel (2009), as many as 8 percent of adolescents attempt suicide, an increase by 300 percent over the last thirty years. Girls make more attempts at suicide, but boys complete suicide four to five times as often as girls. Other studies show that only 7 percent of suicide victims had been receiving mental health care at the time of their death.

Many cases of youth depression go unnoticed. But the symptoms can be evident since depression affects a child's physical, cognitive, and emotional well-being. For example, a child with depression between the ages of six and twelve may exhibit fatigue, difficulty with schoolwork, apathy and a lack of motivation, oversleeping, social isolation, acting out in self-destructive ways, and a sense of hopelessness. Clinical depression is the most common diagnosis of children in a clinical setting (40 to 50 percent of diagnoses). Children and teens who are considered at high risk for depression disorders include those referred to a mental health provider for school problems, those who have medical problems, are pregnant, gay or lesbian, live in rural places (more so than urban settings), get into trouble with the law, or have a family history of depression.

A certain degree of mood swings are normal for adolescents. After all, mood is dependent on hormones, and adolescents are going through normal developmental stages in which their hormone balances are changing. So a child could be totally out of control of his moodiness (mothers know what that feels like when they are pregnant or going through menopause). Knowing such biological causes, he can't be blamed. But he can learn some degree of control over mood swings. And if your child shows signs of depression, it may not just be hormonal; there could be other serious reasons for feeling down.

Exercises

1. Go over these signs of depression with your child. First ask if he feels this way at all (answers "yes"). Then ask, on a scale of zero to ten, with zero being not at all and ten being a lot, or very often, how often:

Q: Do you feel down in the dumps?

Q: Do you have trouble sleeping?

Q: Has your appetite changed: you are either not hungry at all or hungry all the time?

Q: Have you lost interest in doing what you used to like to do?

Q: Have you been neglected or abused?

Q: Have you suffered losses or traumas?

Q: Have you felt like hurting yourself?

Q: Have you felt like life is not worth living?

If your child answers "yes" to any of these questions, you should explore why he feels that way and what could be bothering him. If he answers "yes" to any of the last four questions, you should consult a professional therapist immediately. If the answer regarding severity is over five for any of the first four questions, you should also consult a professional.When depression lasts more than a few days or is accompanied by feelings of doom or despair, it's serious.

2. Ask your child to list the activities or people who make him feel joyous. Now list the things that bring him down and make him feel blue. Ask what you can do to help him feel better.

Lesson: I can get help for my blue mood.

– 18 –

Moving my body

– 18 –

Moving my body

If your child is a "couch potato," of course you're upset, knowing that exercise is important for physical as well as mental fitness. It is particularly important for adolescents to exercise since their bodies are changing, making this a perfect time for them to start good habits.

Research shows that active children, when compared with inactive children, are healthier: they weigh less, have lower blood pressure, and have higher levels of heart-protective lipoproteins. Even though heart attack and stroke are rare in children, evidence shows that the process leading to those conditions begins in childhood. According to the American Heart Association, children in the United States today are less fit than they were a generation ago. Many are showing early signs of cardiovascular risk factors such as physical inactivity, excess weight, higher blood cholesterol, and cigarette smoking. A fitness testing program sponsored by the Chrysler Fund Amateur Athletic Union, which tracks fitness among 9.7 million people between ages six through seventeen, shows that children are becoming slower in endurance running and getting weaker. In addition, the National Health and Nutrition Examination Study (NHANES, 1999–2004) found that the prevalence of overweight American adolescents ages twelve to nineteen was 17.9 percent for males and 16.0 percent for females, with an increase from 1971 to 2004. Blame part of inactivity on the "boob tube" (37.2 percent of high school students spend three or more hours a day watching TV) and on too many hours surfing the Net. Inactive children are more likely to become inactive adults. A healthy lifestyle should start in childhood, including regular physical activity.

If you suggest exercising, your child may object with "I'm too tired," or "I'm too busy." Get around this resistance by encouraging them to start with short and simple activities.

Exercises

A five-minute routine in the morning before going to school will do the trick. The routine should include stretching. For the routine to be more interesting, explain movements relevant to familiar activities. Repeat each sequence twice.

1. Start in a standing position. Reach arms up to the sky, rise up on tiptoes, and flip fingers (as if about to shoot a basketball). Slowly bend slightly backwards (not losing balance), then slowly reach forward and bend down, dropping and letting the head and arms dangle. Return to a normal standing pose.

2. Explain this stretch as if pulling a bow and arrow.

Stretch the right arm out to the side with pointed fingers, reach the left arm out to reach it and draw the left arm across the shoulder as if pulling a bow. Reverse sides.

3. Explain this exercise as if doing a dance step (e.g., ballet): In a standing position, bend the left knee slightly and reach the right leg out in front. Sweep the right leg around to the back as far as possible and back to the front, and return to standing position. Reverse sides and repeat.

4. Yoga is a good technique to do with your child. More children are doing this activity. Go to a yoga class in your neighborhood. Remember to breathe while moving: breathe in through your nose and exhale from your mouth. Allow yourself to relax.

Lesson: Moving my body feels good physically and mentally.

~ 19 ~

Keeping my word

— 19 —

Keeping my word

President Abraham Lincoln was known for being "Honest Abe." The wooden puppet Pinocchio's nose got longer the more lies he told, and a fairy promised he could become a real boy if he would be truthful. Such examples in history and fiction explore the value of honesty. Surveys also show people admire this character trait most in others when making a decision about a close relationship.

According to research studies by Bronson and Merryman (2009), an overwhelming number of young people have told a lie—behavior that increases in frequency as they get older. Only one-third of three-year-olds lie, but over eight out of ten four-year-olds have told a lie, and even more six-year-olds.

Some parents let lies go, hoping it's just storytelling and that their child will change over time. But experts find that kids don't grow out of lying—they get better at it.

Telling the truth will serve your child at this age in establishing a good habit, and also in every aspect throughout his life—friendships, relationships at school, and ultimately, marriage and career.

Teach your child that commitment and keeping your word is important since your word is one of the most precious things you can give to another person and to yourself. Your child can make promises to herself (for example, for personal growth or health, like getting more sleep), to others (that she will help you clean up), or to a group (her sports team or class group working on a project). Breaking agreements destroys trust and confidence, leading others to believe you are dishonest and to avoid you.

Teachable moments

What gets in the way of being honest? It's important to get to the bottom of why your child would tell a lie. Often, children lie to please adults or to not disappoint parents when they know they've done something wrong. Get to the bottom of the reasons for the behavior: Is he afraid of making someone angry at home, being criticized, or admitting something that he will be punished for? Teach him that it is better to tell the truth, because, as Shakespeare penned, "Oh what a tangled web we weave when first we practice to deceive." Lies eventually get found out, which creates a worse situation. It is better to face the music. Being truthful is also a lesson in being responsible.

To start a conversation about whether your child has lied about something, explain or ask, "It's better to tell me what happened," "What are you afraid will happen if you tell the truth?" "Are you afraid that I'll get angry or will scream at you, or even that you are afraid to tell me that you are angry with me?" Explain that being honest with himself comes first! Assure him that you want to know the truth, not just what he thinks you want to hear. Also, teach your child the worth of honesty just as much as you teach the negative consequences of lying.

Suppose your twelve-year-old son hasn't returned a book to the library after repeated reminders, and keeps giving excuses about why he couldn't do it—essentially being dishonest. Tell him, "There are no excuses!" Brainstorm solutions: either make the time to return the book, or ask someone else to help by dropping it off on the way to another place.

Everyone knows the phrase "cold feet" to signify someone who is afraid to make commitments. Ask your child why someone would be scared to keep their word.

Exercises

1. Watch court shows on TV together and point out

how people swear to tell the truth, the whole truth, and nothing but the truth. Explore the unique Web site devoted to truth, www.americanswhotellthetruth.org. Watch CNN Anderson Cooper's show and note how he uses the tagline "Keeping Them Honest." Discuss what that means.

2. Go over lessons about honesty in your child's history book; for example, why was President Lincoln called Honest Abe?

3. Teach your child the importance of keeping agreements. Start with familiar lessons, like those they are learning in Social Studies class. For example, turn to the pages in the textbook about countries that have made agreements, for example, about trade or borders. Discuss current news events about countries signing agreements, such as those dealing with climate change. Talk about what your child is learning about such pacts, what it means for countries to agree, and what happens when they break their

agreements. Then ask what it means when people make agreements and what happens when they don't live up to their end. It can be as simple as your child and her friend agreeing to go to the movies, but the friend calls and cancels. Inevitably, your child feels bad, unimportant, and disappointed. If it happens repeatedly, how does your child feel? Undoubtedly, she feels discouraged and distrustful, and more likely to make a generalization that nobody can be trusted.

Discuss what happens when your child breaks an agreement. How does this affect both himself and the friend? Tell him to put himself in his friend's shoes, and ask him how not keeping his word affects his friend. Ask, "How do you feel about yourself when you don't keep your word?" "What are the consequences?" Possible answers: "I feel bad about myself," "I can't be trusted," and "I might not have any friends anymore."

Being honest in childhood sets the stage for the future, that no matter what they do in life, they know it's important to do what they say they are going to do and to be punctual for someone in their school, job, and elsewhere. Emphasize how commitment will be essential for their future love relationships, including marriage, to work out well and to last.

4. Make an agreement: Write down an agreement that your child can make as an example (such as babysitting his younger sister Saturday night). Write it down on paper to make it more real and ensure that he lives up to it. Track the progress of the commitment and appreciate when it is completed. For example:

My commitment:

I agree to (fill in what you promise to do) with (fill in who or what) by (fill in the date you will finish).

5. Celebrate making—and keeping—commitments. President Clinton does just that in his Clinton Global

Initiative. CGI brings together world leaders, religious icons, nonprofit organizations, philanthropists, and celebrities to help solve the world's most challenging problems. These workshops and meetings are now also held for youth. At CGI University, college students, organizations, and administrators come together to make partnerships and commitments on topics of importance to their generation of youth, such as education, peace, ending poverty, and assuring global health.

Being honest and keeping your commitments also means you are trustworthy and responsible, so see the other chapters and exercises on these topics.

Caution

Don't let honesty go too far! Honesty can be taken to an extreme, such as when people blurt out a truth that is hurtful to others. Your child needs to know not to go too far. For example, if your daughter's friend has a weight problem and your child blurts out, "Gosh, that dress doesn't fit right at all since you put on all that weight!" you can be sure the friend will be devastated. It may be true, but it's a good example of when honesty goes too far.

Lesson: Telling the truth and keeping commitments feels good.

~ 20 ~

Being responsible

~ 20 ~

Being responsible

Being responsible means that you admit, or "own up to," what you have said or done, and it also means you get things done without being asked and are taking control of your own life. Responsibility is indispensable to high self-esteem. The opposite—being irresponsible—implies that you are cannot be trusted or that you are helpless, giving over power to others. Being responsible also means that you know the right thing to do, and you do it.

Exercise

To tell whether your child is being irresponsible, answer the following questions:

Q: Does your child blame others when she does something wrong?

Q: Does your child make excuses whenever he doesn't do something he was supposed to do (for example, "I couldn't walk the dog because the leash wasn't where it was supposed to be")?

Q: Does your child explain his or her behavior by what you do (for example, "How can I be happy when you and daddy are not happy")?

If you answered "yes" to these questions, then you need to concentrate on helping your child become more responsible.

Teachable moments

1. Explain that no one makes you feel a certain way: they may do things that you don't like, but how you respond is up to you. Your responses determine whether you can be responsible.

2. Point out the benefits of being responsible: that

you're reliable, and that people feel they can depend on you, especially in an emergency.

3. When your child does something responsible, appreciate it and point out how exhilarating the experience can feel. Emphasize how being responsible can give you more control over your own life.

Modeling

Model responsibility yourself. Check with the chapter about being on time, since these qualities overlap. You're providing a good example of responsibility if you told your son you would pick him up from school to take him to his baseball game or take your daughter to her piano lesson, and you are there as you said you would be.

Lesson: Step up to the plate and do the right thing.

~ 23 ~

Being real

− 23 −

Being real

Lots of young kids think they have to behave a certain way in order to be accepted by parents and friends. This might make them act in a way that is phony. But being true to oneself and being "real" is key to self-esteem.

Being real means being who you really are. According to psychologist Abraham Maslow's theory, the highest state of achievement is one of being authentic, behaving in a way that is consistent with your deep feelings.

Teachable moment

Tell your child that it's normal sometimes to be scared about letting others know what she really thinks or feels, or who she really is deep inside. Exposing her true feelings to others can leave her vulnerable to their judgment. But remind her that you love her for who she really is inside.

Exercise

Ask your child to close his or her eyes, take a deep breath, inhaling and exhaling. On the next breath, he should inhale and exhale very slowly, concentrating on the breath, really feeling the air filling up his lungs on the inhale and them blowing out his mouth for the exhale. On the next breath, allow him to concentrate on what it feels like inside his body. It may seem different at first, but practicing a few times provides the sense of what it feels like inside to be truly "you."

Lesson: I'm proud of who I am.

~ 21 ~

Being embarrassed by my parents

— 21 —

Being embarrassed by my parents

It's normal for adolescents to be embarrassed by their parents; after all, they're going through a natural stage of being self-conscious about themselves, so they're going to be sensitive to all your attributes or flaws too. Basically, they're afraid of being judged by their friends and coming up short. Once you accept that this is a normal stage of adolescent development, you won't take it so personally and get angry, defensive, or hurt. It doesn't matter if you're brilliant, attractive, or charming—expect your youngster to be embarrassed by you. Your daughter may want you to drop her off three blocks from school so she can walk the rest of the way rather than be seen getting out of your car. Your son may not want to sit next to you in the movies when you go with his friends because you laugh too loudly, and people may turn around to look at you. Or your child may be ambivalent: your son may want you to see him play soccer but cringe if you cheer too loudly and make a spectacle or stand out from the crowd.

Teachable moment

Tell your child to consider another mindset: my parents are not me. I accept them for who they are, and I want them to accept me. If my friends judge me poorly based on how my parents look, talk, or behave, then they're not good friends.

What triggers you?

Don't get lost in your own ego. Realize that your child's feelings are really not about you. Don't argue, insist on your way, or get offended. Give them the space they need to grow and be independent.

Lesson: Parents are their own people.

− 22 −

Expressing appreciation

− 22 −

Expressing appreciation

The Japanese have a favorite therapy called Nai-kan during which you sit in a room alone for hours on end for several days and say "thank you" to everyone and everything out loud. Your child can do a scaled-back version for just two minutes a day, or whenever the mood strikes.

In the fields of finances, accounting, and assessive possessions (like property, land, homes), appreciation relates to the increased value of an asset in contrast to depreciation, which traces its fall in value over its normal lifetime. This process of such "appreciation" presents difficulties when ascribing a value to any particular asset because of the varied interpretations that can be applied, and various instruments and methods that could be used in the valuation process. In a psychological sense, however, appreciation reflects recognition of value, and expression of gratitude, admiration, or approval.

Teachable moment

A powerful story of appreciation tells of a student who remembered a teacher from third grade who influenced his life tremendously, and he sought her out to send a letter saying how much he valued her. The letter found its way to her, and she wrote back that although she was in her eighties, no one had ever told her that and she would cherish it forever. When she died, he saw his letter lying on her chest in the coffin, showing how much the gesture of appreciation meant to her.

Exercises

1. Tell your child to sit in a quiet room with no distractions and concentrate on important people in his

life and how they have contributed to him. Have him start with his mother, going through all the small and seemingly taken-for-granted, as well as significant, ways she has helped him. He should say aloud, "Thank you, mother, for feeding me when I was a baby," "Thank you, mother, for tucking me into bed when I was a child." Then go through the same process with a teacher: "Thank you for teaching me about the Civil War." "Thank you for correcting my homework." Then repeat this process in relation to a friend: "Thank you for inviting me to your house for your birthday party." "Thank you for helping me with my homework."

2. Encourage him to thank or compliment a person directly. Telling people aloud what he likes about them or what they have done for him or anyone else makes him feel good about himself. This also makes the other people feel good! And it further encourages him to repeat positive behavior.

3. Be specific and immediate to notice after he has done something pleasing to you. For example, acknowledge when he says to a friend: "How nice that you picked up that piece of paper you dropped and threw it in the garbage," or when he says to his dad, "Thanks for helping Mom put the dishes away; that teaches me what to do."

Lesson: I thank everyone who enriches my life.

– 24 –

Getting contact comfort

– 24 –

Getting contact comfort

Three hugs a day is the prescription for good health and happiness. "Contact comfort" refers to the positive effects of being held. It's a proven psychological principle that comforting and loving touch makes babies grow healthier, and it applies to health and happiness for all age groups.

Warm embraces also stimulate the healthy "feel-good" body chemicals, like endorphins (the "pleasure chemical") and oxytocin (the "cuddle chemical"), which induce calm and comfort.

If you've ever wondered about the value of contact comfort, just think about how babies get attached to their blankets or their teddy bears and hug both, especially when going to sleep in an unfamiliar or new situation. In a classic social psychology experiment done decades ago, American psychologist Harry Harlow studied mother-child relationships and separation by experimenting with rhesus monkeys, proving the importance of caregiving for social and cognitive development. Two groups of baby monkeys were removed from their real mothers. The first group was exposed to a figure covered in terrycloth that provided no food and a figure made of wire that provided milk in an attached bottle. In the second group, a terrycloth mother provided food while the wire mother did not. The results showed that the young monkeys clung to the terrycloth mother whether food was provided or not. These results suggest that contact was even more important than feeding.

Further, whenever a frightening stimulus was introduced into the cage, the monkeys ran to the cloth mother for protection and comfort, even if that mother did not provide food.

Monkeys in an unfamiliar room clung to their cloth mother surrogate until they felt secure enough to explore. This reaction was in contrast to those monkeys with the wire mother or no mother figure who froze in fear, cried, crouched down, or sucked their thumbs, or ran around searching for the mother figure, crying and screaming. Monkeys raised by the wire mother had more physical problems, like diarrhea and difficulty digesting milk, than those raised with the cloth mother. These experiments provided more evidence that physical closeness and softness was crucial for healthy growth and social, emotional, and intellectual adjustment. The results also proved that nursing was more important for intimate body contact than for food, and that avoiding body contact—in efforts to not spoil a child—is unhealthy.

Harlow's experiments showed the importance of touch and love. He also believed that contact comfort could be provided by either mother or father, a revolutionary idea at the time that is now more widely accepted.

Following Harlow's pioneering work in developmental touch research, further experiments with rats provided evidence that touch during infancy resulted in the decrease of steroid hormones involved in stress. Researchers found that even short-term interruption of the mother-pup interaction in rats significantly affected biochemical processes in the developing pup: it reduced cell growth and differentiation as well as growth-hormone release in various body organs (such as the heart, liver, and all parts of the brain, including the cerebrum, cerebellum, and brain stem); and it increased stress-producing secretion. Additionally, animals deprived of touch and grooming in the first six months of life had weakened immune systems and stress-induced activation of the pituitary-adrenal system, which in turn leads to increased cortisol, a hormone associated with stress. Researchers suggest that regular and natural stimulation of the skin may moderate these dangerous responses in a positive, healthful way.

Teachable moments

1. Explain that "good touches," in which someone is expressing caring with no expectations of a particular response, are healthy, teach you about love, and make you feel warm and cozy. In contrast, "bad touches" make you feel icky and sticky, like someone is demanding a reaction, and even worse, they may be abusive.

2. Hug your child three times a day. A quick embrace will suffice, since some adolescents, particularly boys, may cringe when you go to touch them (normal reactions at their age when they feel awkward about touching).

Caution

Adolescents need to know that hugs and loving touch does not have to lead to sexual behavior—just to reassurance and kindness.

Lesson: Three hugs a day keeps the doctor away.

~ 25 ~

Exercising self-control

— 25 —

Exercising self-control

Self-control is the ability to control emotions, desires, and behavior. An interesting study used marshmallows to test four-year-old children for self-control. The children were each given a marshmallow and told they could eat it any time they wanted, but if they waited fifteen minutes, they would receive another marshmallow. The study's long-term results showed that those who could control their urge to immediately eat the marshmallow correlated well with success in later life.

Adolescents can have raging emotions, partly due to hormonal changes. But some emotions are not appropriate within specific contexts, a distinction they can learn over time and also with your guidance.

Exercise

Have your child fill in the blank while thinking about times when self-control is necessary: I feel like I want to _____, but I think I better not, because _____. (For example: I feel like I want to scream, but I think I better not, because it will upset the people around me; I feel like I want to eat that piece of chocolate cake, but I think I better not because it has too much sugar that isn't good for me.)

Caution

Be aware that self-control is very involved in eating disorders, which present serious problems for this particular age group. A lot of girls, and an increasing number of boys, have eating disorders because they are looking for a way to control their lives. This is important for parents to know, because girls at a younger and younger age are now exhibiting signs of eating disorders.

Lesson: I can control my emotions and behavior.

– 26 –

From sloppy to neat

– 26 –

From sloppy to neat

You know a mess when you see it! When your child's room is in disarray, when he drops things all over the floor and furniture, and when he leaves dirty dishes all over the house, he's being sloppy. If you're a neat freak, this behavior will drive you even more crazy. Your child may just have a sloppy room, or he may disregard being neat and orderly in everything he does—in other words, he has sloppy habits. The goal, of course, is to become more neat, orderly, and systematic.

Choose your battle. You're entitled to insist on neatness for the commonly shared living space, but decide how much energy it's worth to argue or nag about how your child keeps her own room. It may be better to decide that her room is her territory and let her be responsible for it. Also, realize that many kids have messy rooms, and sometimes they grow out of it and become more orderly as they grow up. If you're a neat freak, don't expect too much order from others; what seems like chaos to you may be your child's own system of knowing where things are—that only what's in front of her face is what she can attend to, and once it's out of sight, it's out of mind. Your way is not the only way.

Teachable moment

Ask your child about her reasons for making a mess. Does she feel overwhelmed? Does she want help (are you willing to spend an afternoon teaching her how to be more organized, making files, folding clothes, and putting books in a row)?

What triggers you?

Are you sloppy in your own habits? If you want your child to clean up his or her room, set a good example and have your own room, closet, or kitchen drawers orderly.

Lesson: I'm responsible for my own mess.

~ 27 ~

Being compassionate

— 27 —

Being compassionate

Compassion is a human emotion of understanding, or sympathizing with, the feelings of others, particularly their pain, and the desire to alleviate their suffering. But you can also have compassionate feelings for yourself.

Teachable moment

All religions emphasize compassion, but one leader most renowned for his promotion of such caring is the Dalai Lama, who has become the symbol of compassion. Remind your child of the Golden Rule: Do to others as you would have them do to you.

Exercise

1. Walk a mile in another person's shoes. Describe a situation to your child and ask him or her to imagine being the other person and seeing how that person would feel.

2. Go to the site about the Charter for Compassion, www.charterforcompassion.org, where people are submitting their comments about how to be accepting of others.

What triggers you?

Look inside yourself and examine your own attitudes towards pain and others' suffering.

**Lesson: I have
a heart for myself and others.**

– 28 –

Overcoming prejudice

— 28 —

Overcoming prejudice

It's all too easy for adolescents to make judgments, because they are so self-conscious about being in the in-crowd or the out-crowd. It's common for this age group to start developing cliques. According to psychology theory, intolerance, prejudice, and discrimination can start at this age, as young people struggle to establish their identity and rely on belonging to a group to help them do this. But this need to be part of a group can also lead to some positive outcomes, such as team affiliation, religious affiliation, school affiliation, or even gender identification (as a male or female).

Social psychology theory (the "contact hypothesis") notes that working with others on a project reduces prejudice. In other words, if you "break bread" with someone you may think is different from you, you begin to feel more alike and closer to them.

Exercises

1. Sit down with your child and describe different groups and their characteristics: for example, what are boys like and what are girls like? Do you think that boys are meaner than girls and girls are more kind than boys? How are these groups different and how are they similar? Finding the common ground helps train your child to see that groups have similarities that create a firmer foundation for tolerance.

2. Create opportunities to expose your child to other races, religions, ethnicities, and classes of wealth. If there is a theater group or a team sport in your neighborhood where children of different cultures participate, have your child join.

What triggers you?

As a parent, what prejudices do you have? Do you think men are all cheaters and women are victims? These views about groups can be transmitted to your child.

**Lesson: We are all different
and we are all the same.**

~ 29 ~

Being resourceful

– 29 –

Being resourceful

Being resourceful means being able to act effectively or imaginatively, especially in difficult situations. That means knowing what to do, who to go to for help, or how to make the most of a situation. Resources can be your own abilities that you may not have realized you have, or people or organizations that can help you.

Teachable moments

1. Teach your child that nothing is unattainable once you calmly think about resources you can draw upon.

2. There is nothing wrong with asking for help. In fact, the opposite is true: drawing on your resources

shows intelligence and strength. People are more often than not willing—and happy—to help when they are asked.

3. Help is always available. Knowing that gives your child trust that they are not alone and that people can be counted on.

Exercises

1. Have your child decide on a dilemma; for example: How do I get my bike fixed? Who can help me? Whom do I know who also has a bike that might need to be fixed? I can call the store and ask who they know fixes bikes. Or I can go on the Internet and google "bike repair."

2. Make an extensive list of resources that can help. That includes you, as the parent, as well as other family members, friends, or organizations. Of course, the most popular resource today is the Inter-

net. Encourage your child to use different ways to find out about a topic on the Web. For example, to research for an essay about soccer or to find out why movies about vampires are so popular, use different words to bring up information from sites, or add the word "scholar" to searches to find more academic sources.

3. Go through your child's address list together (as long as she agrees) and put notes next to the names about what they do and how they can be helpful with a certain activity or problem. For example, "What about Aunt Elena who was a philosophy major in college? Let's ask her about Socrates," or "Your friend's mother wears nice jewelry, so maybe she knows where to get that necklace you want," or "Brady's dad is always watching football when I'm at his house, so maybe he can get me a ticket to a game."

Lesson: I can always find the answer.

~ 30 ~

Being a good sport

— 30 —

Being a good sport

W all know that youth playing sports builds character: it teaches them to learn to do their best, cooperate well with others, and determine how to handle being a gracious winner and loser. All of that bodes well for higher self-esteem. With so many more young girls playing team sports these days, learning how to be a good sport is that much more relevant to developing self-esteem for all adolescents.

Teachable moment

Sportsmanship is being a gracious winner and a gracious loser. In sports, there is always a winner or loser. Of course, the winner might feel superior or feel better after the game than the loser, but it is the loser's challenge to feel he or she has played well and is motivated to develop skills even more diligently to play better next time. The classic lesson for young people in playing sports is: "It doesn't matter if you win or lose; it's how you play the game that counts." Of course, winners get more headlines, drafts to professional teams, and millions of dollars at that level, but for most kids, playing the game is a way to train them to do their best, challenge their limits, and test their emotional strength to be able to compete while putting the outcome in perspective (for example, losing without falling apart or unleashing anger).

If you daughter loses in a beauty pageant, rather than become a terrorizing mom who critiques her daughter's performance ("You should have turned more like I showed you," "The other girl won because she had a much prettier costume and voice than yours"), boost your child for having the confidence to perform and for doing her best. Criticism

would make her deflated and emotionally trauma-
tized, and lead to blaming herself for letting you
down and being a failure. Point out everything she
did that was excellent so she can know what to re-
peat next time. You can say, "Your dance steps in the
second stanza were perfect." This approach builds
her self-confidence.

Exercise

Get your child involved with a sport or other
competitive activity she would enjoy. This can be
field hockey, dancing, or martial arts. Discuss to-
gether what it means to perform at your best, and
also what it means to perform up to your own stan-
dards, not just about winning the competition and
beating the other contestants. Ask what she consid-
ers a "good" performance. Ask, "Which is more
important to you: doing your best, or getting first
place?" Her focus should be on doing better and bet-
ter in her own performance rather than comparing

herself to others, so that she develops an inner sense of pride in what she is doing more than an outer sense of beating the other person.

What triggers you?

Look back into your past to when you played sports or even competed in some event such as a debate. How did you handle your own performance compared to that of others, as well as the final score? Your own maturity in these situations will spill over into your children's tendencies. For example, if you always begrudgingly said, "I could have won the triathlons I competed in at your age if it weren't for that burly guy, who I am sure was taking drugs to make him faster." Such a reaction means you are begrudging your loss and not presenting a good example to your child of how to accept an outcome. Rather say, "I had such a good time competing in races when I was your age. It felt so good to be testing myself to be my best."

Lesson: It doesn't matter whether I win or lose; it's how I play the game.

~ 31 ~

Feeling empowered

− 31 −

Feeling empowered

Empowerment is currently a buzz word that signi-fies utilizing personal and social resources to take control of your destiny. Youth groups and work-shops, including those called "Empower Now," de-veloped by Dr. Judy, are meant to do activities that help train participants to make choices that bolster their internal strength and confidence to accomplish what they want. In this way, self-esteem is key to the process of empowerment.

To empower a group of people means giving them the feeling that they are able to accomplish something. Some research has even been done to clarify what this phrase means and how to create a sense of empowerment in individuals, groups, and communities. Teaching your child personal empowerment helps him further to become active in the community, allowing him to grow in social contexts. The empowered child feels good about himself by noticing his contribution to the greater good and by being an agent of potential change.

An exercise to create a sense of empowerment

One good way to feel empowered is by doing a physical exercise that gets you in touch with how you can control the energy in your body. Share this four-step exercise with your adolescent (from the "Empower Now" workshops) for moving his energy to experience empowerment:

1. Activation: Get really active, moving your body and making noises as loudly as you like, moving arms up and down—just to amplify energy.

2. Stop and be quiet. You can stand still or lie on the ground. While you're silent, concentrate on the

energy in your body. Feel any twitches, tension, or even electrical charges.

3. Reactivate by beginning to move slowly, feeling how much power you have in your body. Increase the movements, adding arms and legs. Take a deep breath as if you are inhaling air all the way from the bottom of your feet up into your heart, tracing the air going through your body, imagining it going into your head then back into your heart. In essence, you are circulating the power energy through your body.

4. Active play: Now you can let your body and mind run freely by moving however you like. This exercise gets you in touch with your body, your energy, and your inner self.

Another exercise to feel empowered

Have your child bring his arms out to the side bent upwards at the elbow and really flex the muscles in his arms (feeling the strength). Then have him breathe in and bring his hands close to his heart, saying "I have a good heart." Tell him to feel the muscle in his arm and say, "I am powerful," "I am strong," and then bring his arms in close to his heart and say, 'I am loving, I am loving." This mixture of heart and strength create empowerment.

Lesson: I am empowered to be whatever I want to be.

Notes